Deliverance Ministry Basic Training

Learn How To Cast Out Demons & Set The Captives Free

I.R. Womack

Copyright © 2015 I.R. Womack

I.R. Womack

P.O. Box 894

Edgewood, MD 21040

CONTENTS

CHAPTER 1

WHAT IS DELIVERANCE MINISTRY?

The initial thought that comes to the mind of many people when they hear the word 'deliverance' is the casting out of demons from an individual's life. This perception is right, to an extent, but it falls short of a comprehensive description. In the New Testament, there are two primary Greek words for deliverance. The first is *aphesis* which means deliverance from bondage or imprisonment. The second is *soteria* meaning salvation or deliverance from the molestation of enemies. The essence of the ministry of deliverance, then, is bringing God's people out of any form of bondage, into the freedom and victory that our Lord Jesus Christ died to give them on the cross. The casting out of demons is merely a component (albeit, an often necessary one), in the all-encompassing ministry of deliverance.

It is indisputable that quite often; deliverance ministry is necessitated by overt demonic influence and control over a person, making them manifest such behavior that it is evident to all who observe them that something is wrong. On the opposite side of the spectrum, the effects of demonic infestation can be much more subtle, requiring the grace and anointing of God to detect it.

With the understanding that the casting out of demons is one component of deliverance ministry, there are other essential elements that must be addressed, albeit in brief, in order to give proper context to the topic:

Inner Healing

This is when a person has an emotional wound that needs healing, usually as a result of having been rejected, abused, hurt or wounded in some way. Demons will attempt to exploit these wounds and use them as entry points, granting them access to the inner workings of the person's life and thereby facilitating their eventual demonization. The healing of these inner wounds is a vital aspect of the process of restoration in the lives of individuals seeking to be fully delivered. The goal of this inner healing is not to forget the event that caused the wound, but rather, to be healed of the pain, trauma or ungodly emotions such as bitterness, hatred and unforgiveness that's plaguing the soul as a result of the event. It is nearly impossible for a person to experience total and lasting deliverance, if these emotional wounds are not properly dealt with.

Tearing Down Strongholds

Over time, demons are able to feed people with enough lies and deceptions to get them into incorrect and ungodly patterns of thought. These mindsets are *strongholds*. They need to be torn down in order to facilitate deliverance and enable the individual to begin living in total freedom. Failure to tear down such strongholds during the deliverance process, not only impedes the successful completion of the deliverance, but gives demons a basis on which to hang around and continue tormenting or manipulating the individual.

Removing Legal Rights

More often than not, the demonization of a person's life is as a result of certain factors that have given the demonic entity a legal right to be there. As the name implies, the rights are legal, and brute force will often not work against them, making it necessary to accurately determine the source of these legal rights. This is a vital step in the facilitation of the deliverance process.

Casting Out Demons

This element is where it all culminates; the expulsion of demons from the life of a person, so that the person can live free from the influence and control of satan and his minions. This particular element has been a major source of the confusion surrounding the deliverance ministry, and it will be further addressed and given more details in this book.

It is important for you to understand that deliverance ministry is not a ministry that is embarked upon by virtue of a person's title, whether in the church or outside. Deliverance ministry is part of our inheritance in Christ Jesus. It is not something one person can claim to have and another person complains of not having. The rule is that as long as a person is a believer, then he/she has the duty and authority to carry on the ministry of deliverance wherever and whenever the need arises. With proper training, any Spirit-filled believer can minister deliverance successfully to someone that is in need.

Deliverance Ministry Is Miracle Ministry

Therefore they that were scattered abroad went everywhere preaching the word. Then Philip went down to the city of Samaria, and preached Christ unto them. And the people with one accord gave heed unto those things which Philip spake, hearing and seeing the miracles which he did. For unclean spirits, crying with loud voice, came out of many that were possessed with them: and many taken with palsies, and that were lame, were healed. And there was great joy in that city." (Acts 8: 4-8 KJV)

He said to them, "Go into all the world and preach the gospel to all creation. Whoever believes and is baptized will be saved, but whoever does not believe will be condemned. And these signs will accompany those who believe: In my name they will drive out demons; they will speak in new tongues; they will pick up snakes with their hands; and when they drink deadly poison, it will not hurt them at all; they will place their hands on sick people, and they will get well."

(Mark 16: 15-18 NIV)

The first passage describes Phillip's evangelistic work in a city of Samaria. It is very clear that Phillip's performance of miracles was a crucial factor in the success that he was able to achieve there. The Bible says that they gave heed to the words that he said, after having heard and seen the miracles, which he did. The casting out of demons features as the first type of miracle to be mentioned, underscoring the pre-eminence of the deliverance ministry as will be discussed later.

In the second passage of Scripture, Jesus Christ commissioned the twelve apostles to go out into the world and preach the gospel. The first sign that he made mention of that would accompany them was the casting out of demons. By these passages of Scripture, we understand that Jesus Christ established the ministry of deliverance as an essential and preeminent work of the Kingdom.

<u>NOTES</u>

_____

_____

_____

_____

_____

_____

_____

_____

_____

_____

_____

_____

_____

_____

_____

_____

_____

_____

_____

_____

_____

_____

_____

_____

Chapter One Review Questions

1. What are the two primary Greek words for 'deliverance' in the New Testament?

2. Define the two primary Greek words for deliverance.

3. List three components of deliverance ministry other than casting out demons.

4. With proper training, who is qualified to do deliverance ministry?

5. Is deliverance ministry a miracle ministry? Explain.

6. Describe the term 'legal right' as it pertains to deliverance ministry.

7. What is a 'stronghold'?

8. What are some steps discussed in this chapter that a deliverance minister should take to facilitate the process of casting out demons?

9. What is likely to be the result of casting out demons from a person's life without ever addressing the emotional wounds that caused

the demonization?

10. Name at least three emotional wounds that can lead to the demonization of an individual if not properly dealt with.

CHAPTER 2

CAN A CHRISTIAN BE POSSESSED BY A DEMON?

A lot of controversies have been generated over the question of whether or not a Christian can be possessed by a demon. This question has engendered an age-long debate among scholars, theologians and church leaders as to the possibility of a believer being under the control of a demon, or being possessed by one. With my understanding of the many scriptures related to this issue, coupled with my personal experience as a deliverance minister, I conclude that a Christian cannot be *possessed* by a demon. However, a Christian can be afflicted, tormented, or even controlled by a demon, thereby necessitating the ministry of deliverance to bring him/her into the freedom that is his/her inheritance in Christ.

Although the Bible does not make specific reference to a "Christian" having a demon, there are multiple instances where it describes "believers" having demons. Fundamentally, those two terms are the same, and as such, it goes to reason that although a Christian's life can be affected by a demon to various degrees, this is quite different from being possessed by demons. The word 'possess' denotes ownership. Every person who has come into covenant with God through Jesus Christ is considered by God to be His possession and therefore cannot be possessed by demons.

"For you are a people holy to the Lord your God. Out of all the peoples on the face of the earth, the Lord has chosen you to be his treasured possession." (Deuteronomy 14:2 NIV)

"Do you not know that your bodies are temples of the Holy Spirit, who is in you, whom you have received from God? You are not your own; you were bought at a price."

(1 Corinthians 6: 19-20 NIV)

Christians have been purchased by the blood of Jesus Christ, and are therefore, His possession. The word 'Lord' comes from the Greek word *kyrios* meaning master or owner. When Christians call Jesus their Lord, they are acknowledging the fact that He is their possessor.

Some of the contentions and divisions on the subject of demons possessing Christians stem from how the translators of the King James Version translated the Greek term "*daimonizomai*". The word "possessed" as they have translated it, is actually not the most accurate one for reasons already mentioned. *Daimonizomai* actually means to be *under the power of a demon*. Scriptures that mention a person as being "possessed" by a demon would be better rendered as "demonized", "have a demon", or "under the power of a demon".

With this said, although a Christian cannot be possessed by a demon, he/she can, most certainly, be afflicted, tormented, influenced, manipulated, and to various degrees, be controlled by demonic entities. Being *under the power* of a demon then, would present in the same manner as what some consider as being *possessed*, which more accurately describes the matter.

Another area of contention and debate is whether a demon can control born again Christians from the inside or outside of their bodies. Those who believe that it is not possible for a Christian to have a demon on the inside of them contend that the Holy Spirit and demons cannot occupy the same place and therefore, a true Christian cannot possibly have a demon residing on the inside. I do not subscribe to this doctrine. I believe that a proper understanding of the Scriptures that deal with this matter will make evident that although the Holy Spirit and demons cannot occupy the same space, this doesn't take away the fact that an individual can have the Holy Spirit residing in one dimension of their inner being and still have a demon residing and controlling them to some degree from another. Demons can inhabit and afflict a person's physical body such as the bones, muscles, organs, respiratory system, etc. (see Mark 9:25), or the soul (mind, will and emotions). Here is my explanation:

The word *spirit* in the New Testament is translated from the Greek word *pneuma*. This is the essence of man. This term can also be translated as *breathe* or *wind*. This pneuma is that Breathe of the Almighty God which He blew into Adam. It is also that aspect of our inner being that can perceive divine things (1 Corinthians 2:14).

Although some people use the terms 'spirit and soul' interchangeably, they actually come from two different Greek words in Scripture. The word for soul in Greek is *psyche*. The psyche is comprised of the emotions, mind and will. Man is a triune being (1 Thessalonians 5:23). He is a spirit that has a soul, and lives in a body. Whereas at salvation, the Holy Spirit regenerates and resides in the spirit dimension (John 3:6), it is the realm of the soul (emotions, mind and will), or the physical realm (various areas within the physical body), where demons can afflict or control a person from the inside.

This is why Paul could address born again Christians in Philippians 2:12 and tell them to work out their *salvation* with fear and trembling. If they were already saved, then what is there to work out? Paul understood that at the initial salvation experience, it was the spirit that was immediately delivered from the power of sin, satan, and demonic influence. However, the soul's salvation (freedom from the influence and effects of the enemy in one's emotions, mind, and will) was something that needed to be *worked out* over time.

I must be very clear, even if the soul is not completely delivered from the influence and effects of the enemy; the soul is still saved in the sense that the individual's soul will still make it into Heaven. After all, this is why Jesus died on the cross. Our souls are saved by grace through faith, and not our works. However, the soul being saved in the sense of being completely liberated from all the influence and power of the enemy is something that must be worked out over time. I think any Christian can agree that they are still a *work in progress.*

Here are a few Scriptures that confirm my point of view pertaining to satan or demons occupying believers from the inside:

But a certain man named Ananias, with Sapphira his wife,

sold a possession, And kept back part of the price, his wife also being privy to it, and brought a certain part, and laid it at the apostles' feet. But Peter said, Ananias, why hath Satan filled thine heart to lie to the Holy Ghost, and to keep back part of the price of the land?

(Acts 5: 1-3 KJV)

Ananias was a believer who was a part of the Jerusalem Church. However, in verse three, Peter said that satan had "filled the heart" of Ananias. The word heart is translated from the Greek word *kardia* which means soul, mind, will and character. Through the sin of greed and idolatry, satan had gained legal right to manipulate and influence Ananias' mind and will.

Then Simon himself believed also: and when he was baptized, he continued with Philip, and wondered, beholding the miracles and signs which were done...And when Simon saw that through laying on of the apostles' hands the Holy Ghost was given, he offered them money, Saying, Give me also this power, that on whomsoever I lay hands, he may receive the Holy Ghost. But Peter said unto him, Thy money perish with thee, because thou hast thought that the gift of God may be purchased with money. Thou hast neither part nor lot in this matter: for thy heart is not right in the sight of God. Repent therefore of this thy wickedness, and pray God, if perhaps the thought of thine heart may be forgiven thee. For I perceive that thou art in the gall of bitterness, and in the bond of iniquity. (Acts 8:13; 18-23 KJV)

Verse thirteen of Acts chapter eight explicitly states that Simon the sorcerer became a believer and was baptized. However, in verses 21-23 Peter discerns that Simon's heart is not right with God and that he is full of bitterness and in captivity of sin. It's apparent that although Simon became a believer, he was still demonized and in need of much deliverance.

"Then entered Satan into Judas surnamed Iscariot, being of the number of the twelve."

(Luke 22:3 KJV)

Here we don't see a demon, but satan himself who entered into Judas. He was a believer, disciple, and apostle of Jesus but his evil inclinations opened a doorway and gave legal right for satan to enter and control him to do his bidding.

But I am afraid that just as Eve was deceived by the serpent's cunning, your minds may somehow be led astray from your sincere and pure devotion to Christ. For if someone comes to you and preaches a Jesus other than the Jesus we preached, or if you receive a different spirit from the Spirit you received, or a different gospel from the one you accepted, you put up with it easily enough. (2 Corinthians 11: 3-4 NIV)

Here, we see the apostle Paul addressing Christians at the church of Corinth. This passage of Scripture makes it quite evident that although a Christian can receive the Holy Spirit, it is still possible to receive *another* spirit if they are not careful and on guard.

It must be noted that, although those who claim Christians cannot have demons are wrong, and they, for the most part, make that contention in sincere faith and with the conviction that it is true, the refusal to accept that Christians can have demons may actually have some very harmful effects on Christians, both individually and as a body:

- The false doctrine is perpetuated that all problems and travails are due to "lack of true surrender."

- Hopelessness is fostered within the demonized people.

- Bad personality traits and habits are thought to be

a matter of nature and are therefore, unchangeable.

- Inherited characteristics are similarly thought to be unchangeable.

- Medical diagnosis and medication take precedence over the authority and power of God.

NOTES

Chapter Two Review Questions

1. Can a Christian be 'demon possessed'? Explain.

2. Define the term "*daimonizomai*".

3. Can an evil spirit manipulate or control a born again believer from the inside of him/her? Explain.

4. What are some harmful effects of refusing to believe that a Christian can be demonized?

5. Since born again believers are already 'saved', why did Apostle Paul tell them in Philippians 2:12 to work out their salvation?

6. According to Acts chapter 8, did Simon the sorcerer become a genuine believer?

7. After Simon became a believer, was he still in need of deliverance? Why?

8. According to 2 Corinthians 11: 3-4, is it possible for a Spirit-filled believer to receive *another* spirit?

9. According to the author, what legal right did satan have to fill the heart of Ananias?

10. Did satan manipulate Ananias from the inside or the outside? Explain.

CHAPTER 3

THE PREEMINENCE OF DELIVERANCE MINISTRY

The principle is well established, that where the Bible gives a list of things, they are usually in order of importance, starting from the most important and preeminent.

In Matthew chapter 10, Jesus Christ conferred authority upon his disciples to drive out evil spirits, and to heal diseases and sicknesses. The essential thing for you to note in this passage is that the power to cast out evil spirits was the first authority and mandate that Jesus Christ gave to his disciples, even ahead of healing the sick and preaching the gospel.

Further evidence lies in Mark 16:17 NIV, "*And these signs will accompany those who believe: In my name they will drive out demons; they will speak in new tongues.*"

Here again, the deliverance ministry is the first to be mentioned, thereby emphasizing its position as a central point of Jesus' ministry, and very dear to the heart of God. This is understandable when one looks at it from the perspective of how God must feel when some of the people whom He sent His Son, Jesus Christ to die for on the cross are perpetually under the control and influence of demons. Also, the Greek word for salvation translates literally to deliverance, and this further underscores this preeminence that the ministry of deliverance has.

You must note here however, that deliverance ministry is not restricted to pastors, church leaders or other titled positions within the church. It is also not a gift of the Spirit that one person has but is absent in another person. Deliverance ministry, especially the aspect of casting out demons, is an inherent authority of every believer. This general availability is another manifestation of the preeminent nature of deliverance ministry, as it underscores the fact that it is too important a function to be left to the chosen few. If the apostle or pastor is not around someday when demonic manifestations are occurring in the home of a believer or elsewhere, he or she should be well trained and equipped to take them on, bind them, and cast them out.

The Impact Of Deliverance Ministry

- **It grabs attention**

Deliverance ministry is one of the most effective ways to get people to sit up and listen to what you have to say because it is natural for people to be attracted to unusual things that transcend the ordinary and day to day experiences. In the work of ministry, this is very important because quite often people are either just not willing to listen to the gospel, or are listening with an indolent attitude. Miracles will definitely catch the attention of people when they see, or hear of it, and this can go a long way to streamline the path of the gospel into their hearts. As a case study, let's take a second look at Phillip's ministry in Samaria:

"Those who had been scattered preached the word wherever they went. Philip went down to a city in Samaria and proclaimed the Messiah there. When the crowds heard Philip and saw the signs he performed, they all paid close attention to what he said. For with shrieks, impure spirits came out of many, and many who were paralyzed or lame were healed. So there was great joy in that city." (Acts 8: 4-8 NIV)

Had Phillip not performed the signs and wonders he did, starting with the casting out of demons, would people still have listened to him as intently as they did? We do not know and cannot say for sure, but what is clear from that verse is that the miracles that were performed by Phillip went to a great extent in making his voice heard in his proclamation of the gospel of Christ. As ministers of God, it is imperative that you follow this example and put more focus on your deliverance ministry to give that extra effectiveness to the preaching of the gospel.

If you practice, or have practiced street evangelism, you will agree with me that nothing increases the likelihood of a person accepting Christ into his/her life more than a prayer before asking them. You might not be aware though, that that prayer is a sort of deliverance ministry on its own, albeit, a subtle one. Sometimes, when you approach people to commit their lives to Christ, they are unresponsive, either because they don't have time, they are too busy or they simply just don't want to hear what you have to say. Often, these reactions are not wholly of their own volition, but a result of demonic influence that is preventing them from appreciating the joy and grace they stand to enjoy in Christ. Upon praying with them (not many people will refuse a simple offer to pray for them, their family, or particular need), you will often find that their hearts are much more receptive to the gospel, and some may even give their lives to Christ.

- **It brings Joy**

Another impact of deliverance ministry is the joy it brings into the hearts of those people who are touched by it, whether directly or indirectly. Speaking with people who have recently been delivered will give you a sense of the immeasurable relief, happiness and joy that people experience when the yoke of the devil is lifted off them; the oppressions they have suffered over time have become memories and they can look forward to living a life in the liberty and grace of God. This joy transcends just the individual because the deliverance of one person usually has a great impact on not just the person's life, but that of his/her family and community.

When a person is delivered from evil spirits of lust, addiction or anger, it might be that the person's marriage has been saved, by virtue of that. Again, Acts 8:4 says that after the signs and wonders that Phillip performed in Samaria, "there was great joy in the city", telling us essentially, that deliverance ministry can even extend to covering a whole city in the joy of the Lord. If deliverance can bring joy to a person, a family, a community and even a city, how is it that it cannot bring that same joy to a nation, or the whole world?

Related to this is the fact that it strengthens the church, as the Bible says: *"the joy of the Lord is your strength"* (Nehemiah 8:10). When the Church is free from demonic oppression, influence or control, it stands to reason that they will be able to pursue the ministry of Christ more effectively and thoroughly. The effect of demonic presence on a person or church is terrible. Demons can bring about the collapse of a strong and vibrant minister of God and the ministry they have built over time, effectively dealing another blow to the work of the gospel. For this reason, it is imperative that all measures, including deliverance, are taken to remove the influence of demons in the Church, the body of Christ.

NOTES

_____

_____

_____

_____

_____

_____

_____

_____

_____

_____

_____

_____

_____

_____

_____

_____

_____

_____

_____

_____

_____

_____

_____

_____

_____

_____

Chapter Three Review Questions

1. In Mark chapter 16, what was the first authority and mandate given to the disciples by Jesus?

2. Is the ability to cast out demons a gift of the Spirit?

3. How was deliverance ministry a central point of Jesus' ministry?

4. Casting out demons is an inherent authority of every believer. True or False?

5. How can an individual's deliverance impact a group of people or even an entire city?

6. How is prayer connected to deliverance ministry?

7. How does deliverance ministry strengthen the church?

CHAPTER 4

NECESSARY WEAPONS FOR CASTING OUT DEMONS

In this chapter, we'll take a look at those things that must, of necessity, be in place to ensure that deliverance is carried out successfully.

Authority of the Believer

Knowledge is power. In deliverance ministry, one of the most important things is for you to understand who you are, and your position in the spiritual scheme of things. Only by doing this will you begin to embrace and operate on the level of power and authority that Christ has vested in you. It's an unfortunate reality that even people with degrees and titles in the body of Christ have not come to a full understanding of their power and authority, making them quite ineffective in the ministry of deliverance. The mindset of capability and superior authority is an essential element to casting out demons. You are not supposed to plead with a demon to come out from the person it is oppressing. The correct thing to do would be to give it a command, with full knowledge and assurance that it has no choice but to obey.

"Then came the disciples to Jesus apart, and said, **why could not we cast him out? And Jesus said unto them, Because of your unbelief:** *for verily I say unto you, if ye have faith as a grain of mustard seed, ye shall say unto this mountain, Remove hence to yonder place; and it shall remove; and nothing shall be impossible unto you. Howbeit this kind goeth not out but by prayer and fasting."*
(Matthew 17:19-21 KJV emphasis added)

This verse makes the above point very clear. The disciples had approached the task of casting out the demon with a mentality that did not convey the requisite power and authority to the demon, and it exploited that, leaving them to toil continually without achieving any success in expelling it. What

Jesus Christ told them in essence, was that, had they approached the demon in the way and manner which He did, its occupation of the demonized person would have become a thing of the past. Demons are subject to you by virtue of the authority that Jesus Christ has conferred on you. He has given you the *exousia* (Greek for authority), to tread upon serpents and scorpions.

"Verily, verily, I say unto you, **He that believeth on me, the works that I do shall he do also;** *and greater works than these shall he do; because I go unto my Father."* (John 14:12 KJV, emphasis added)

This verse shows that authority is conferred on God's children, as believers in Christ, to do the things that Jesus did while He was on earth. As a result of this authority, dealing with demons ought not to be an onerous task to be fearful and apprehensive about. Rather, you should face demons as courageously as David, running towards and confronting the enemy in full assurance that victory will be yours.

Spiritual Gifts

The gifts of the Holy Spirit can play a major role in deliverance ministry. My focus will be on discerning of spirits, word of knowledge and the working of miracles.

The gift of discerning of spirits is that which grants you the ability to easily recognize the specifics of the demon that is oppressing the person to be delivered. This recognition is very important because demons cause different types of oppression according to their type, and the process of their removal usually necessitates some specific attack on the particular demon, as opposed to attempting to cast out the generality of demons. If you have some experience in deliverance ministry, you must be aware that knowing the type of the particular demon you are trying to cast out goes a long way in increasing the effectiveness of the deliverance, as it quickly brings the demon to the surface, where it can be summarily cast out from the life of the person whom you are delivering. Not knowing the particulars of the demon you want to cast out will serve to extend the period of the deliverance, increase the toll it will have on the oppressed person and give the demon the opportunity to marshal its strength against you.

The word of knowledge comes into play by giving you prior information and insight into the oppression and demonization of the person involved. This is vital because, even when conducting a thorough interview before deliverance ministry, the oppressed person may not reveal necessary information to you, either out of a sincere lack of knowledge or deliberate concealment. There may be situations you encounter where individuals are not comfortable giving you the information out of shame, fear or guilt. Just as knowing the particulars of the demon occupying the person is important, it is also very important that you, as the deliverance minister, be aware of the specifics and particulars of the oppression in the life of the person and its root causes. This enables you to more effectively lead the person in the process of deliverance. The gift of the word of knowledge fills this gap by revealing things to you that ordinarily, you would have had to do without, leading to a prolonged deliverance process.

The gift of the working of miracles empowers a person to perform miracles by the power of the

Holy Spirit. What this means is that even though deliverance ministry is not one of the gifts of the Spirit and can be performed by any believer in Christ, the presence of the working of miracles enables an individual to expel demons with little effort and without needing to go through all of the steps that a deliverance minister or counselor will usually have to take when acting on authority alone. The gift of the working of miracles essentially adds more *power to the punch* of the deliverance minister. In the book of Acts, there are two prime examples of the effectiveness of the working of miracles in the ministry of deliverance:

*"Nevertheless, more and more men and women believed in the Lord and were added to their number. As a result, people brought the sick into the streets and laid them on beds and mats so that at least Peter's shadow might fall on some of them as he passed by. Crowds gathered also from the towns around Jerusalem, bringing their sick **and those tormented by impure spirits, and all of them were healed.**"* (Acts 5:14-16 NIV, emphasis added)

*"God did extraordinary miracles through Paul, so that even handkerchiefs and aprons that had touched him were taken to the sick, and their illnesses were cured **and the evil**"*

spirits left them."

(Acts 19:11-12 NIV, emphasis added)

c) Faith

The importance of faith to the ministry of deliverance is highlighted in Matthew 17:19-20:

> "*Then came the disciples to Jesus apart, and said,* **why could not we cast him out? And Jesus said unto them, Because of your unbelief:** *for verily I say unto you, If ye have faith as a grain of mustard seed, ye shall say unto this mountain, Remove hence to yonder place; and it shall remove; and nothing shall be impossible unto you.*"
> (KJV, emphasis added)

The failure of the disciples to cast out the demon was attributed by Christ to their lack of faith in themselves and in the power which they carried as sons of God. As a deliverance minister, you must ensure that your faith is never lacking, because it is a determinant of the effectiveness of your deliverance ministry. Thankfully, the Bible has prescribed ways to make sure that our faith levels stay up. This leads to our next two weapons:

d) Fasting and Prayer

"Howbeit this kind goeth not out but by prayer and fasting."
(Matthew 17:21 KJV)

Scripture commands us to be strong in the Lord and in His mighty power (Ephesians 6:10). Fasting and prayer facilitates this by bringing a person closer to God, thereby increasing the level of faith and power that he/she has in the mightiness of the Lord our God. It is apparent from the scripture mentioned above, that certain demons are stronger than others, necessitating the need for the deliverance minister to fast and pray in order to receive the power required to expel them.

e) The Sword of the Spirit

In Matthew chapter 4, Jesus Christ was taken into the wilderness to be tempted by the devil, and he used the word of God as a weapon to defeat the temptation that the devil thrust at him. This provides an example for what we, as children of God, can achieve with the word of God in spiritual warfare and deliverance ministry. Ephesians 6:17 says:

"Take the helmet of salvation and the sword of the Spirit, which is the word of God." (KJV)

Of all the items mentioned as comprising the armor of God, only the sword is an offensive weapon. This hints at its suitability and the intention of God that it be our recourse when we combat the forces of darkness. During deliverance, it is the word of God, this sword of the Spirit, that you will apply in binding and casting out demons from the children of God who are oppressed.

NOTES

_____
_____
_____
_____
_____
_____
_____
_____
_____
_____
_____
_____
_____
_____
_____
_____
_____
_____
_____
_____
_____
_____
_____
_____
_____
_____
_____

Chapter Four Review Questions

1. What is the significance of a believer having a full understanding of his/her authority to cast out demons?

2. Describe how unbelief can hinder or negate a believer's power to cast out demons?

3. How does the *discerning of spirits* facilitate the casting out of demons?

4. How does the *word of knowledge* facilitate the casting out of demons?

5. How does the *working of miracles* facilitate the casting out of demons?

6. Is faith necessary in order to cast out demons? Explain.

7. Are some demons stronger than others? Explain.

8. How does fasting and prayer facilitate the ministry of deliverance?

9. What is the sword of the Spirit?

10. How is the sword of the Spirit utilized in deliverance ministry?

CHAPTER 5

OPEN DOORS
(Demonic Entry Points)

Demons require an entry point before they can infest a person's life. The entry point is usually created by one or more things that the individual or someone in their bloodline has done, knowingly or unknowingly, which gave the demons a sort of legal right or claim to his/her life. Some of the common open doors/entry points will be discussed below:

Willful Sin: The foremost and most common source of demonic attack, willful and habitual sins are those serious types of sins. Where the sins are being committed with regularity over a long period of time, this increases the seriousness and the likelihood that demons will be able to use them as a gateway into the life of the person. Some examples of sins that constitute demonic entry points include:

1. Criminal activity

2. Drugs

3. Alcohol abuse

4. Lying

5. Adultery

6. Fornication, especially when the partner is demonized.

7. Heavy verbal, physical, or sexual abuse on someone

The Occult: The occult is another area that is a major draw for demons, providing a large pool of people to infest, beginning from those who just try one or two times, experimenting. The demons that are to be found in this area are some of the most difficult demons to cast out, and most likely to engage you in a vicious struggle to retain control of the person they are occupying. The kinds of activities that constitute dabbling in the occult are so varied that some of them are considered by some people to be too minor to carry any risk of negative consequences. This is not true, because over time, we have come to be aware that any sort of involvement with the occult; at whatever level and to whatever extent, constitutes major legal right for demons to launch an attack into a person's life.

Examples of activities associated with occultism are: tarot card reading, ball gazing, seeing psychics, hypnotism, crystals, witchcraft, voodoo, satanism, far eastern meditation, séances, astrology and a host of others, including ouija boards, dungeons and dragons and similar role playing games.

Apart from occultic activities, we must be aware that **cursed objects** also pose a very potent danger of inviting demons into a person's life. Physical objects have the ability to contain and operate spiritual influence; whether Godly or evil. Items such as occultic books, carvings, rings etc., have the capacity to be legal rights in and of themselves, whether a person is aware of their nature or not. These items may have been acquired by the person innocently, not knowing that they have some sort of connection with the pagan culture and belief systems of the places where they are bought from. The only solution to removing this particular legal right is to do away (burn, preferably) with each and every item that you have the slightest suspicion of having an occultic connection:

Deuteronomy 7:25-26 (NIV)

"The images of their gods you are to burn in the fire. Do not covet the silver and gold on them, and do not take it for yourselves, or you will be ensnared by it, for it is detestable to the Lord your God. Do not bring a detestable thing into your house or you, like it, will be set apart for destruction. Regard it as vile and utterly detest it, for it is set apart for destruction."

Acts19:19 (NLT)

"A number of them who had been practicing sorcery brought their incantation books and burned them at a public bonfire. The value of the books was several million dollars."

Generational/Inheritance: We often see cases where children of alcoholics end up becoming alcoholics themselves. This is not mere coincidence, but rather, the result of demons entering the child's life through the bloodline and successfully influencing the child to tread in the parent's path. Demons will search for a family member on whom to transfer the yoke of their domination by getting the other family member to do the exact things that the original person was doing. Demons are often successful at this with children because of the relative ease with which they are influenced by their parents and older family members around them.

In order to block and remove this legal right in a person's life, confession must be made by the person of all the sins that they are aware of that have been committed by any of their ancestors, whether recent or in the past. It may also be necessary for questions to be asked of other family members to determine the root cause and extent of the generational affliction, especially where the same problem has occurred in a suspiciously high number of family members over the years.

Unforgiveness:

"And when you stand praying, if you hold anything against anyone, forgive them, so that your Father in heaven may forgive you your sins." (Mark 11:25 NIV)

Unforgiveness prevents a person from being in right standing with God, as we can see from the verse above. When people refuse to forgive others who have wronged them, it opens a major loophole that demons are always eager to try and exploit. The demons know that because they are not completely on good terms with God, their prayer capabilities are affected and their power in the spiritual realm is reduced.

Once demons have gained access, they do their best to engender and encourage the feelings of bitterness, hatred and spitefulness so as to increase their hold and dominion.

The remedy for this is for the person with bitterness and anger in their heart to make a final, definite choice to let the feelings of resentment go and forgive the person or persons against whom they have been holding grudges. This not only removes the legal right that demons would have banked on to launch their attack, but also, brings the person back within the full protection of God, making sure that their faith and spiritual power are strong enough to resist any attack from demons.

Trauma: When terrible things happen to people, it can release a flood of emotions and feelings in them such as sadness, anger and resentment. Negative emotions and feelings attract demons. In the case of the death of a loved one, divorce, job loss or other extreme trauma, people are often inclined to let their guards down and assume a despondent and fatalistic mind-set which makes them prime targets for demons to launch their attack.

To fend off the possibility of being infested by demons through this particular legal right, the best thing for people going through traumatic experiences is to move closer to God, by spending more time in prayer, studying and confessing his Word, participating more actively in Church activities and talking over the issues with qualified individuals. These things will keep their minds occupied and focused on God and His ability to solve any problem, no matter how difficult it may seem. This stops any demon attempting to come into their minds and manipulate it, right in its tracks.

Abuse: Abuse of whatever form, whether verbal, physical or sexual can be a very potent legal right that opens doors for demons to come into a person's life. Where abuse has occurred, demons quickly move in and try to take over both the abuser and the person they have abused, on the basis of the gravity of the sin that the abuser has committed, and the feelings of resentment and hate that the abused may harbor in his/her heart in that particular period of time.

Curses: Curses are a major conduit for demons to take up residence in a person's life. There are three types of curses that demons often ride on to infest their victims:

Direct Curses: This type of curse results when a person with an occultic power places a curse on another person directly, for whatever reason. The efficacy of this type of curse is usually dependent on the position of the person that has been cursed in the eyes of God. The Bible says that a curse cannot take effect on a person if there is no cause

(Proverbs 26:2). This implies that where there is a cause, a curse that has been placed on a person will take effect in his/her life. What happens is that where there is no just cause for the curse that has been sent against someone, the protective hedge that the person has with God completely blocks and stops the curse from proceeding into the person's life. However, where there is a just cause that validates the curse, the hedge is comprised and can allow the curse to take effect in the person's life, bringing the demons attached to it along.

When a person has had a curse sent against him/her, he/she must first be guided through an honest appraisal and evaluation of his/her life, especially his/her relationship with the person responsible for the curse. This will help to determine if indeed, there is a cause that has granted permission for the curse to operate in his/her life and given legal rights to demons to afflict them.

Word Curses: These curses are usually the results of careless or malicious statements made by people about others, oblivious of the level of impact that they may have on the person to whom they are directed. When people take the evil words of others to heart, they can develop negative emotions and even begin to believe the lies. If not properly dealt with, it can become a stronghold that demons can exploit and then begin to work on actualizing the curse.

Self Inflicted Word Curses: Another type of curse that can create a route for demons to get into a person's life, is a curse that is self-inflicted. These arise from constant negative confessions about self; telling him/herself that he/she is not good, will never amount to anything, is too fat, ugly or will never get someone to love him/her, etc. Apart from doing very serious damage to a person's sense of self-worth and self-confidence, this type of thinking can hinder a person from coming into full actualization of his/her potential in the natural and spiritual realms.

Indulging in this type of self-destructive behavior invites demons to begin flocking around such a person and attempting to plant further evil thoughts in such a mind, along the lines of the denigrating things that the person has been saying in his/her mind or verbally all along. If the person begins to agree with the things that the demons have been putting in his/her mind, then a door is opened for demons to enter the person's life and begin their operation there.

When you come across someone whose demonization is as a result of self-cursing, then what you should do is get his/her mind renewed with the word of God about him/herself as a person, and his/her position in Christ. You should put the Scriptures to use in convincing the individual of the love that God has for him/her, and the plan and purpose He has for his/her life. After this, you can begin the other necessary steps to cast the evil spirits out of the person's life.

Ungodly Soul Ties: Often, when dealing with some of the legal rights discussed above, the issue of ungodly soul ties will come up, making it an aspect that you want to particularly pay close attention to when trying to investigate the probable causes of a demonic affliction in a person's life.

Soul ties are not necessarily bad; sometimes, they can actually be good. The good soul ties are those that engender a Godly and healthy spiritual bond with a person, bringing them closer in the spiritual realm than ordinary earthly affiliation can account for. Soul ties ought to exist between husbands and wives, parents and their children, siblings and close friends. An example of a good soul tie can be seen in the friendship that came into being between Jonathan and King David. It is stated clearly in the Bible, specifically 1 Samuel 18:1, that their souls were knitted to each other, and that they "loved one another as their own soul."

As opposed to this healthy, beneficial type of soul tie, there can also be soul ties that are ungodly and unhealthy. An area where this type of soul tie is commonly seen is in the area of abuse; where the person who is committing the abuse is trying to manipulate and control the person that they are abusing. This often leads to a situation where the person being abused begins to live in fear of the abuser and begins to try to keep the situation under control by obliging the abuser in order to please him/her. This is futile most of the time, and only results in a circle of violence where the abuser continues with the abuse to such an extent and for such a period of time that the person being abused finally snaps and breaks away.

Doing that doesn't bring an end to the matter though, as demons will often try to exploit the situation and attempt to attach themselves to the person who has been abused. Their legal right in these instances is usually unforgiveness or fear.

False Religions: There is only one way to God, and that is through His Son Jesus Christ, who came to earth and sacrificed Himself on the cross for the salvation of mankind. There are many other religions and belief systems out there that preach different things, but that is only because they were set up by satan and his agents, including the demons which in many cases explains the demonic affliction that besets some of the adherents of those false religions. Since they hold beliefs, and participate in rituals that were prescribed by evil spirits, those forces automatically gain a foothold in their lives.

Any person coming from such a background must be willing to convert and accept Jesus Christ as his/her Lord and Savior. That is the only way by which they can hope to gain deliverance from the demons that are plaguing them. Refusal to renounce the false religion that they were members of, acts as a proclamation of their allegiance, therefore validating the presence of the demons in their lives.

In order for such individuals to proceed with the process of getting delivered, they must first renounce and withdraw their allegiance to the false religion that they previously belonged to. Then, you can begin to engage the demons in battle, making it clear to them that the factor that previously granted them an invitation into their lives has been replaced by a relationship with Jesus Christ.

<u>NOTES</u>

_____
_____
_____
_____
_____
_____
_____
_____
_____
_____
_____
_____
_____
_____
_____
_____
_____
_____
_____
_____
_____
_____

Chapter Five Review Questions

1. What is a demonic entry point?

2. List a few occultic activities that are demonic entry points.

3. Why do you suppose demons that are attached to a person's life through occultic activities are some of the most challenging to cast out?

4. Does an individual have to be knowledgeable of the fact that they are engaging in an occultic activity in order for demons associated with the activity to demonize him/her? Explain.

5. Can evil spirits be attached to physical objects? Explain.

6. When a cursed object has been identified, what should an individual do with it? Give at least one Scripture to support your answer.

7. Can a demon enter into a person's life through his/her bloodline? Explain.

8. How is unforgiveness a demonic entry point?

9. What is a self-inflicted word curse?

10. How is false religion a demonic entry point?

CHAPTER 6

COMMON DEMON GROUPINGS

"Then Jesus asked him, "What is your name?" "My name is Legion," he replied, "for we are many."
(Mark 5:9 NIV)

From Jesus' encounter with the demon who called himself Legion, we can deduce two things. Firstly, demons are identifiable by their nature. Secondly, demons will often work in groups in order to fortify their stronghold in an individual's life. As stated earlier in this book, knowing the names of the demons you are dealing with will greatly facilitate the deliverance process. In their classic book, "Pigs In The Parlor", Frank and Ida Mae Hammond present a list of fifty-three demon groupings that is very helpful in identifying the strongman and underlings of a particular demonic infestation. The list is as follows:

1. **BITTERNESS** – Resentment, Hatred Unforgiveness, Violence, Temper, Anger Retaliation, Murder

2. **REBELLION** - Self-will, Stubbornness Disobedience, Anti-submissive

3. **STRIFE** – Contention, Bickering, Argument, Quarreling, Fighting

4. **CONTROL** – Possessiveness, Dominance, Witchcraft

5. **RETALIATION** – Destruction, Spite, Hatred, Sadism, Hurt, Cruelty

6. **ACCUSATION** – Judging, Criticism Fault-finding

7. **REJECTION** - Fear of Rejection, Self rejection

8. **INSECURITY** – Inferiority complex, Self-Pity, Loneliness, Timidity, Shyness, Inadequacy, Ineptness

9. **JEALOUSY** – Envy, Suspicion, Distrust, Selfishness

10. **WITHDRAWAL** - Pouting, Daydreaming, Fantasy, Pretense, Unreality

11. **ESCAPE** - Indifference, Stoicism, Passivity, Sleepiness, Alcoholism, Drug addiction

12. **PASSIVITY** - Funk, Indifference, Listlessness, Lethargy

13. **DEPRESSION** – Despair, Despondency, Discouragement, Defeatism, Dejection, Hopelessness, Suicide, Death, Insomnia, Morbidity

14. **HEAVINESS** – Gloom, Burden, Disgust

15. **WORRY** – Anxiety, Fear, Dread, Apprehension

16.NERVOUSNESS - Tension, Headache, Nervous habits, Restlessness, Excitement Insomnia, Roving

17.SENSITIVENESS - Self-awareness, Fear of man, Fear of disapproval

18.PERSECUTION – Unfairness, Fear of judgment, Fear of condemnation, Fear of accusation, Fear of reproof, Sensitiveness

19.MENTAL ILLNESS - Insanity, Madness, Mania, Retardation, Senility, Schizophrenia Paranoia Hallucinations

20. SCHIZOPHRENIA (See Chapter 21 of *Pigs in the Parlour*)

21.PARANOIA – Jealousy, Envy, Suspicion, Distrust, Persecution, Fears, Confrontation

22. CONFUSION – Frustration, Incoherence, Forgetfulness

23. DOUBT – Unbelief, Skepticism

24. INDECISION - Procrastination, Compromise, Confusion, Forgetfulness, Indifference

25. SELF-DECEPTION - Self-delusion, Self-seduction, Pride

26. MIND-BINDING – Confusion, Fear of man, Fear of failure, Occultism, Spiritism

27. MIND IDOLATRY - Intellectualism Rationalization, Pride, Ego

28. FEARS (All kinds) - Phobias (All kinds), Hysteria

29. FEAR OF AUTHORITY – Lying, Deceit

30. PRIDE – Ego, Vanity, Self-righteousness Haughtiness, Importance, Arrogance

31. AFFECTATION – Theatrics, Playacting, Sophistication, Pretension

32. COVETOUSNESS - Stealing, Kleptomania, Material lust, Greed Discontent

33. PERFECTION – Pride, Vanity, Ego, Frustration, Criticism, Irritability, Intolerance, Anger

34. COMPETITION - Driving, Argument, Pride, Ego

35. IMPATIENCE – Agitation, Frustration, Intolerance, Resentment, Criticism

36. FALSE BURDEN – False responsibility, False compassion

37. GRIEF – Sorrow, Heartache, Heartbreak, Crying, Sadness, Cruel

38. FATIGUE – Tiredness, Weariness, Laziness

39. INFIRMITY - (May include any disease or sickness)

40. DEATH

41.INHERITANCE - (Physical) (Emotional) (Mental) (Curses)

42. HYPER-ACTIVITY - Restlessness Driving, Pressure

43. CURSING – Blasphemy, Coarse jesting, Gossip, Criticism, Backbiting, Mockery, Belittling, Railing

44. ADDICTIVE & COMPULSIVE - Nicotine, Alcohol, Drugs, Medications Caffeine, Gluttony

45. GLUTTONY – Nervousness, Compulsive eating, Resentment, Frustration, Idleness, Self-pity, Self-reward

46. SELF-ACCUSATION - Self-hatred, Self-condemnation

47. GUILT – Condemnation, Shame, Unworthiness, Embarrassment

48. SEXUAL IMPURITY – Lust, Fantasy lust, Masturbation, Homosexuality, Lesbianism, Adultery, Fornication, Incest Harlotry, Rape, Exposure, Frigidity

49. CULTS - Jehovah's Witnesses, Christian Science, Rosicrucianism, Theosophy, Urantia, Subud, Latihan, Unity, Mormonism, Bahaism, Unitarianism (Lodges, societies and social agencies using the Bible & God as a basis but omitting the blood atonement of Jesus Christ)

50. OCCULTISM - Ouija Board, Palmistry Handwriting analysis, Automatic handwriting, ESP, Hypnotism, Horoscope, Astrology, Levitation, Fortune telling, Water witching, Tarot cards, Pendulum, Witchcraft, Black magic, White magic, Conjuration, Incantation, Charms, Fetishes, Etc.

51.RELIGION – Ritualism, Formalism, Legalism, Doctrinal obsession, Seduction Doctrinal error, Fear of God, Fear of Hell, Fear of lost salvation, Religiosity Etc.

52. SPIRITISM – Séance, Spirit guide, Necromancy, Etc.

53. FALSE RELIGIONS – Buddhism, Taoism, Hinduism, Islam, Shintoism, Confucianism, Etc.

NOTES

_____
_____
_____
_____
_____
_____
_____
_____
_____
_____
_____
_____
_____
_____
_____
_____
_____
_____
_____
_____
_____
_____

Chapter Six Review Questions

1. Are demons identifiable by their nature? Explain.

2. Do demons prefer to work alone or in groups? Give a Scriptural reference for your response.

3. What is the advantage of understanding demon groupings?

4. Which demons are associated with gluttony?

5. Which demons are associated with sexual impurity?

6. Which demons are associated with paranoia?

7. Which demons are associated with indecision?

8. Which demons are associated with jealousy?

9. Which demons are associated with control?

10. Which demons are associated with retaliation?

CHAPTER 7

PREPARING FOR BATTLE

Be Always Ready

"Be alert and of sober mind. Your enemy the devil prowls around like a roaring lion looking for someone to devour."
(1 Peter 5:8 NIV)

As a deliverance minister, it is imperative that you are always alert and ready to deal with demonic issues and deliver people from under their yokes. You may not always have prior notice of what is going on, i.e., the demonic activity that will necessitate your stepping in to deliver someone. The Bible tells us to put on the whole armor of God. This advice is particularly apt in deliverance ministry, to avoid being caught unawares. You must make sure that it is not only when the time to conduct a deliverance is approaching that you get to putting on the armor of God, or meditating on the word of God to sharpen your sword. It should be that you are continually keeping yourself fit in the spirit and ever-ready to deal with any situation that may arise. However, when you do have knowledge of a serious spiritual battle that lies ahead, it is beneficial to go the extra mile.

"Keep this Book of the Law always on your lips; meditate on it day and night, so that you may be careful to do everything written in it. Then you will be prosperous and successful."

(Joshua 1:8 NIV)

Prayer and fasting are essential parts of the Christian lifestyle, but as it is with the word of God, when preparing for deliverance, there ought to be an exceptionally high amount of prayer and fasting to ensure that our spirits are ready and able to tackle the challenge ahead.

"And pray in the Spirit on all occasions with all kinds of prayers and requests. With this in mind, be alert and always keep on praying for all the Lord's people."
(Ephesians 6:18 NIV)

"And He said to them, "Because of the littleness of your faith; for truly I say to you, if you have faith the size of a mustard seed, you will say to this mountain, 'Move from here to there,' and it will move; and nothing will be impossible to you. "But this kind does not go out except by prayer and fasting." (Matthew 17: 19-21 KJV)

In the latter passage of Scripture, Jesus Christ was admonishing the disciples for their lack of faith, but further study seems to show that Christ was connecting the inadequacy of their faith with their lack of prayer and fasting, implying that if they had prayed and fasted, they would have had sufficient faith to drive out the demon that was opposing them.

A crucial part of your preparation for deliverance sessions should be a review of the questionnaire that the person in question should have filled out, detailing the root cause and specifics of the demonization in their lives. This review will give you an overview of the issue so that you have a solid idea of what you're about to face, and can prepare accordingly.

If you are conducting deliverance ministry in a situation where reviewing a questionnaire is not feasible, such as during a service or a conference, then it is important to do a brief interview with the individual in order to gain the information needed to conduct deliverance ministry as efficiently as possible. In many cases, especially during a full blown demonic manifestation, it is not possible to conduct even a brief interview with the demonized individual. You may have to deal with the demons first and then conduct the interview as part of the post-deliverance process.

<u>NOTES</u>

Chapter Seven Review Questions

1. The proper time to put on the whole armor of God is after a situation has been identified that necessitates spiritual warfare. True or False. Explain.

2. As it relates to deliverance ministry, what is the significance of meditating on the word of God day and night?

3. How does prayer and fasting fortify one's faith?

4. According to the information provided in this chapter, how can a deliverance minister determine the root cause(s) of a particular demonization?

5. If you are in a situation that necessitates deliverance ministry but it is not feasible to have the individual fill out a questionnaire, what can you have the person do to help facilitate the deliverance process?

6. Why is it important to be alert and of a sober mind?

7. Have you ever been in a service where there was a demonic manifestation and the leaders of the church were not aptly prepared to deal with it? Explain?

8. Have you ever witnessed a severe demonic manifestation outside of a church service? Was there anyone around to deal with it? Explain.

9. 1 Peter 5:8 states that the devil "prowls around like a roaring lion seeking for someone to devour." How does this affect your resolve to be *ready* at all times?

10. Name at least three ways stated in this chapter that will help a trained believer to be ready and able to minister deliverance to a demonized person at any given time.

CHAPTER 8

EIGHT STEP DELIVERANCE MINISTRY MODEL

As a deliverance minister, it would be gravely unwise to make knee jerk decisions and begin to bind and cast out demons without having taken some necessary preparatory steps, as well as having in mind a definite agenda on how the deliverance will proceed. With deliverance, the planning and preparatory stage is almost as important as the actual deliverance itself. This initial stage is where the deliverance minister becomes equipped with the knowledge of what exactly he/she is aiming to deliver the demonized person from, enabling him/her to form a plan of action, the proper implementation of which will assure success by the grace of God. In this chapter, we'll go through an eight-step model for a successful deliverance.

Step #1

Find Out What the Bondages Are

"What do you want me to do for you?" Jesus asked him. The blind man said, "Rabbi, I want to see."

(Mark 10:51 NIV)

"So they brought him. When the spirit saw Jesus, it immediately threw the boy into a convulsion. He fell to the ground and rolled around, foaming at the mouth.

Jesus asked the boy's father, "How long has he been like this?"

"From childhood," he answered. "It has often thrown him into fire or water to kill him..."

(Mark 9: 20-21 NIV)

Deliverance is most effective when the entirety of the bondage and oppression being suffered by the person is laid bare, enabling the deliverance minister to know what exactly the demon is afflicting the person with; the specific manifestations and precise demon groupings that the person's affliction fall into. This makes it possible for the minister to get to know exactly which demons are occupying the person, and form a plan on how to get the demonized individual free. Apart from knowing the details of the oppression, it is imperative at this stage for you to get to know the exact root cause of the oppression. Demonization does not happen without cause. There is always a door that has been opened or a hedge that has been breached that allows it to take place. For there to be an effective deliverance, the root cause must be exposed and properly dealt with.

Attempting to deliver a person without determining the root cause of the demonization would amount to trying to kill weeds by cutting them off at the top, or even at the middle. As long as the roots are intact, it will grow back, in all probability bigger and stronger than before.

"When an impure spirit comes out of a person, it goes through arid places seeking rest and does not find it. Then it says, 'I will return to the house I left.' When it arrives, it finds the house unoccupied, swept clean and put in order. Then it goes and takes seven more spirits more wicked than itself, and they go in and live there. And the final condition of that person is worse than the first…"

(Matthew 12:43-45 NIV)

This chilling account is what is likely to be the end result of a deliverance that is conducted without the requisite investigation being done into the background of the person, as well as the proper follow up with the individual after he/she has been delivered. Knowledge is power. The more power you operate with, in deliverance ministry, the more likely that the demonized individual will become and remain totally free.

In order to achieve this objective of full knowledge of the facts, I suggest that a form be prepared for people seeking deliverance, with questions designed to bring the details of their demonization to the fore. The form must collect such information as what exactly the affliction is as well as its manifestations, whether it is addiction to drugs or alcohol, seizures, sexual immorality or a full blown manifestation where the person periodically gets taken over by the evil spirit. The length of time is very important too, especially when trying to trace the origin of the demonic infestation in the person's life, and whether it is an individual or generational issue.

At this stage, it is extremely important that you gain the trust and confidence of the oppressed person, making sure that your speech and actions embolden them to tell you everything that you need to know. Be extremely candid with them and assure them of your complete discretion and ability to keep what they tell you in confidence. It is equally imperative to utilize any gifts of the Spirit that are at your disposal such as, the gift of the word of knowledge and the discerning of spirits. These spiritual gifts will be very helpful in receiving any pertinent facts and identifying any spirits that are in operation that have not been revealed through the interview.

Step #2

Salvation

When a person is to be delivered, it is essential that if he or she had not been saved before, they become so by the end of the deliverance. This is to avoid the scenario painted by the Bible in Matthew chapter twelve, where a demon goes to find seven more wicked ones than itself, and invites them into the person's life, beginning a new oppression and domination of the person's soul. In this verse, the demon returned to find that the house was empty. Only then did it go to call more demons to come join in the habitation of the house. What this tells us is that the actions of the demon were predicated upon the state it found the house in. If the house had been occupied when it returned, by the same entity that drove it away in the first place, it would not have been able to re-enter.

When ministering deliverance, you must allow yourself to be guided fully by the Holy Spirit as to the most appropriate time for the person to commit themselves to Jesus and become born-again. This is because there is no set-in-concrete rule as to what point exactly in the deliverance process it ought to occur. You will have to make the decision on a case by case basis. Sometimes, it is most appropriate before deliverance, while at other times it should be during the deliverance process. The reason for this is that when a person is under very strong demonic influence, it is virtually impossible for the person to make the decision to come to Christ. The restraining pressure being applied by the demon(s) hinders them from responding to the truth. In such cases, you have to wait until an advanced stage of the deliverance to bring them to Christ.

"If you declare with your mouth, "Jesus is Lord," and believe in your heart that God raised him from the dead, you will be saved." (Romans 10:9 NIV)

The point of this verse, in relation to deliverance ministry is that at a certain point, the person to be delivered must come to Christ, otherwise, there won't be any lasting deliverance as the demons will resume their occupation of the person's life in the near future.

Step #3

<u>Forgiveness</u>

This is another element of the deliverance process that must be put in place for the deliverance to actually turn out completely successful. When a person is harboring bitterness, malice or hatred against someone, the deliverance process is impeded, and naturally so, considering that demons and their powers thrive in that sort of environment. As a deliverance minister, you ought to guide a person's mind and heart along the path of forgiveness by getting them to open up to you about whatever issues and feelings of ill-will they still harbor in their hearts, and then explain to them that in order to be fully delivered of their oppression, they have to let those feelings go and truly forgive the persons who wronged them, regardless of what was done to them.

Oftentimes, you will come across cases where deliverance takes place automatically as soon as complete forgiveness has been actualized. In those cases, what took place was the coming into effect of anointing that had been released a long time ago, but had not been able to have the intended impact because of the evil thoughts or negative emotions present in the individual's soul.

"And when ye stand praying, forgive, if ye have ought against any: that your Father also which is in heaven may forgive you your trespasses. But if ye do not forgive, neither will your Father which is in heaven forgive your trespasses."

(Mark 11: 25-26 KJV)

This verse highlights the way in which unforgiveness can be a legal ground for demonization. As a deliverance minister, you must make sure to break all legal grounds for demonic oppression of the person seeking deliverance.

Step #4

<u>Repentance and Faith</u>

Over time, repentance has come to mean ceasing to commit a known sin, but in its actual sense, to repent is to change one's mind, to turn one's mind and thoughts from a particular thing. The difference between the two senses in which the word is used is highlighted in the following scripture:

"But when he saw many of the Pharisees and Sadducees coming to where he was baptizing, he said to them: "You brood of vipers! Who warned you to flee from the coming wrath? Produce fruit in keeping with repentance." (Matthew 3: 7-8 NIV)

This makes it clear that there is repentance, and there are the fruits of repentance, which are the corresponding actions that a person takes as a result of the repentance that has taken place in their mind. Many instances can be found in the scriptures where a person made repentance not only for themselves, but for their lineage and forebears. This underscores the importance of repentance in deliverance ministry, where the demonic oppression has come into place as a result of the actions of the person or his parents, grandparents or upwards, repentance must be made accordingly.

Faith would be the catalyst for the coming into place of the fruits of repentance, because in essence, it means turning to God, following His word and

His will, thereby extending to doing or not doing whatever it is that has been repented of by the person. In essence, repentance is turning from sin, and faith is turning to God. It is equally as important to turn to God as it is to turn from sin because one cannot fully turn to God without having turned from sin, and turning from sin without turning to God would essentially amount to sweeping the house clean in readiness for the return of the demon and its seven associates. In essence, when conducting deliverance, you must make sure that the person to be delivered completely repents of any and every sin in his/her life, as well as on behalf of their ancestors. Then, ensure that they have turned to Jesus Christ wholeheartedly before moving on to the next step.

Step #5

<u>Denouncing and Renouncing</u>

"Rather, we have renounced secret and shameful ways..."
(2 Corinthians 4:2 NIV)

To denounce means to publicly declare something to be wrong or evil. To renounce means to give something up or to refuse to obey any longer. After repenting of personal and ancestral sins, the next thing for the person seeking deliverance to do is to denounce and renounce all known sinful activities including demonic covenants, idolatry, cultism, addictions, sinful lifestyles, ect. If these things are not denounced and renounced, the individual's deliverance can be severely hindered.

The person ought to be making vocal statements denouncing the devil and renouncing all his/her works, specifically, by naming the ones that come to his/her mind, and in a general manner. At this stage, the legal rights making the demon(s) to continue occupying the person are being removed by virtue of the denouncements being made by the person, and this is the point where demons usually begin to manifest and cause physical reactions in the person whom they are occupying. Sometimes, this manifestation could be a complete taking over of the person to the extent of controlling his/her every action. The manifestation could also begin in a more subtle way like sudden feelings of anger in the oppressed person, feeling of pain or pressure in a part of the body or screaming and shrieking continuously.

Things to note at this stage include physical preparation; towels and buckets should be made available and easily accessible because often, during the deliverance process, there are bodily secretions of mucus, urine, vomit or even feces. You must make sure that you do not stop treating people with love and care when they get to this stage, regardless of the form their manifestation takes, and refrain from hurting or treating them in a dishonorable way. Some deliverance ministers attempt to make a spectacle by doing humiliating things to the person they are supposed to be ministering to. This type of behavior is contrary to a deliverance minister's purpose and should be avoided at all costs.

Generally, it is very advisable that where possible, deliverance, and especially this stage, should be conducted with a partner. The partner plays the role of support as you minister the deliverance, in case of a protracted session when you get tired, as well as being able to bear witness as to the way in which the deliverance was conducted. This is very good for accountability purposes and prevention of your name, reputation and ministry getting soiled with allegations of misconduct.

Step #6

Use Your Authority

"...Finally Paul became so annoyed that he turned around and said to the spirit, "In the name of Jesus Christ I command you to come out of her!" At that moment the spirit left her."

(Acts 16:18 NIV)

As discussed earlier, in order to effectively cast out demons, the command to cast them out must be authoritative in the utmost sense of the word. The mind-set of capability and assurance that a demon will indeed be cast out when you say so can only come from identifying with Christ and recognizing that your deliverance ministry is not being conducted from the earthly realm alone, but from a heavenly position with Christ. The Bible says that we are the body of Christ, as such, anything that is beneath Christ's feet, like demons, is automatically beneath ours as well.

While renunciation tears up the lease of the demon

in the person's life, the word of authority is necessary to actually evict the demon completely.

In essence, at this stage you must begin to bind and expel the demons. Command the demons to come out in Jesus' Name. (Identifying the *strongman* or head demon of a demon cluster will facilitate this process.) Continue in this vein for as long as is necessary and repeat any necessary steps, until the demons are driven out of the person.

Step #7

<u>Baptism and Infilling of the Holy Spirit</u>

*"Do not get drunk on wine, which leads to debauchery.
Instead, be filled with the Spirit,"*
(Ephesians 5:18 NIV)

After the person has been delivered from the hands of the demons previously oppressing him/her, it is necessary for he/she to receive the baptism of the Holy Spirit. This will help to ensure that his/her mind continues to be occupied with the things of God, and if the expelled demon should return to check out the house, it would find it occupied, without any opportunity of return.

Step #8

Follow up

"Do not conform to the pattern of this world, but be transformed by the renewing of your mind. Then you will be able to test and approve what God's will is--his good, pleasing and perfect will."

(Romans 12:2 NIV)

The end game of deliverance ministry is not the casting out of demons. Rather, it's a transformed life by the renewing of the mind. There is need for a constant renewal of the mind with the things of God and activities that occupy the mind, leaving no room for a relapse.

For lasting deliverance, the delivered person should participate in Christian disciplines and activities such as prayer, fasting, worship and praise of God, fellowship with the saints and Bible Study. Receiving counseling after the deliverance is highly recommendable as well. Whenever possible, the deliverance minister should follow up with the delivered person to ensure that the deliverance was done thoroughly and that proper steps are being taken to maintain the deliverance.

NOTES

Chapter Eight Review Questions

1. List and explain step #1 of the Eight-Step Deliverance Ministry Model.

2. List and explain step #2 of the Eight-Step Deliverance Ministry Model.

3. List and explain step #3 of the Eight-Step Deliverance Ministry Model.

4. List and explain step #4 of the Eight-Step Deliverance Ministry Model.

5. List and explain step #5 of the Eight-Step Deliverance Ministry Model.

6. List and explain step #6 of the Eight-Step Deliverance Ministry Model.

7. List and explain step #7 of the Eight-Step Deliverance Ministry Model.

8. List and explain step #8 of the Eight-Step Deliverance Ministry Model.

9. The *end game* of deliverance ministry is casting out demons? True or False? Explain.

10. What step in the deliverance ministry model had you not considered prior to reading this book? How will this step help you to be a more effective deliverance minister?

CHAPTER 9

CONCLUSION

This course has been a walkthrough of the foundational principles of deliverance ministry. It highlights its preeminent position in the Christian faith as is made clear in the Bible by the ministry and doctrine of Jesus Christ and His disciples. We have established the fact that deliverance ministry is a very crucial precursor to other works of the Kingdom and holds a very prominent position in the eyes of God.

We have seen that although Christians cannot be *possessed* by demons, they can be *demonized* (brought under their power and influence) to varying degrees depending on several factors. We have presented the most common open doors as well as the demon clusters that can exploit them. We've explored the necessary weapons and steps of preparation that you as a deliverance minister, must equip yourself with prior to confronting the forces of evil and casting out demons from an individual's life. As a culmination, you have learned the comprehensive eight-step deliverance model, encompassing the preparatory stages up to the post-deliverance period.

It is my prayer that the teachings you have received in this book, help you to consistently and successfully bring deliverance to God's people from demonic bondages, and into the liberty that is their inheritance in Christ Jesus our Lord!

<u>NOTES</u>

BIBLIOGRAPHY

1. Bible Knowledge, (2010). *Legal Rights of Demons - How to Deal With Them.* [online] Available at: http://www.bible-knowledge.com/dealing-with-the-legal-rights-of-demons/ [Accessed 17 Feb. 2015].

2. Anon,(2015).[online]Available.at:http://www.breadoflifebiblestudy.com/Lessons/14SatansKingdomAndSpiritualWarfare/Articles/BasicDeliveranceManual.pdf [Accessed 17 Feb. 2015].

Made in the USA
Middletown, DE
19 April 2018